Alzheimer's
SUCKS!

MELISSA JONES

QUARTZ RIDGE
PUBLISHING

ISBN#: 979-8-9991018-0-8

Illustrations by Tara Thelen

Design by Deborah Perdue, Illumination Graphics

Dedicated to

Patricia Lou James

Thank you for being an incredible role
model, and teaching by example.
Thank you for being the most honest,
generous person I know, and for showing me
how to be loving, supportive, and always do
the right thing even when it's hard.
You were met with an unfortunate situation,
and you handled it all with grace.

In Memory of

Howard Russell James

The depiction of my father in this book is not
a representation of who he was as a man,
only his final chapter. Previously he was a
vibrant, successful man with a full life. He
served his country in the Air Force, was
active in fraternal organizations, and had a
wonderful, happy family. I wish I could have
gotten to know him better.

CONTENTS

LETTER TO PARENTS

Alzheimer's disease is hard – for everyone. And it's really hard to know how to handle the topic with kids. There's often a tendency for adults to try to protect kids from difficult situations and try to hide the hard, ugly truth. It's difficult to know what to say and it can be uncomfortable to talk about – for both kids and adults.

From my experience, as a child of a father with Alzheimer's, "protecting" the kids by not talking about it is not helpful. Kids need to talk, vent, cry, and ask questions . . . just like adults do. Avoiding conversations won't hide the problem. Kids are perceptive. They will pick up on unusual behavior, and wonder what's going on. It can be very confusing if no one explains the situation. Sit with them, talk with them, share with them. Let them know you are scared and sad and confused too. There is comfort in knowing others share the same feelings you have. Let them see that you are struggling too. Being open and honest will be good for both of you and bring you closer together during the time you're dealing with the disease – and throughout the rest of your lives.

This book is intended to help facilitate the process. Encourage your kids to write in it and express themselves – it is so helpful. (Journaling is helpful for adults too!) If they're willing to share what they write, it will also give you a starting point for conversations. Make it a habit to discuss the situation and your feelings regularly and be sure to share your stories and experiences with each other.

Much love,
Melissa

What is happening!?
My family says something is wrong
but I don't know if I believe it.

I don't remember exactly when my dad was diagnosed with Alzheimer's disease. I think it was a gradual process of my mom realizing there was really something wrong. There's a lot of denial around admitting someone actually has Alzheimer's. No one wants to believe it, and so many things can be explained away in the beginning. I mean, everyone forgets things sometimes, right? But eventually, the occurrences become far too frequent and behaviors change to more than just forgetfulness. A person with

Alzheimer's may start doing completely illogical things like leaving the house with no pants on, or putting ice cream in the cupboard. There comes a point when denial is no longer possible and ignoring the problem can be dangerous.

I remember my mom saying that some of my dad's co-workers came to her in the beginning, telling her about unusual behaviors at work. My dad worked in a manufacturing plant, so mistakes could easily bring harm to himself or others. It wasn't long after that he had to quit working and stay home.

Action:

Do you remember the first time you realized there was something really wrong? What happened that day?

Confused.
I'm seeing crazy things
and don't know what to do.

This is so weird. I'm supposed to be the child but my dad is acting like one. I'm home alone with him and having to act like the adult. It's so uncomfortable. I can't

tell him not to do things, but sometimes what he does is dangerous. I feel like I'm babysitting and can't leave him alone. Today he was hungry and wanted a hot dog. I was so nervous and scared as he started to turn on the stove. He put a pan of water on a burner and put in a hot dog . . . and watched. After the water began to boil, and before I realized what he was doing, he stuck his finger directly in the boiling water to see if the hot dog was hot yet. I don't know if he actually touched the hot dog, but that boiling water was HOT. He jumped back and yelled, and ended up with a severely burned finger. I took care of making his food for him but that's a memory I'll never forget. I think it was later the same day I saw him staring at a cake on the kitchen counter. He wanted a piece but couldn't figure out how to get it, so he used an ink pen as a knife and just cut a square and picked it up and ate it with his hands.

Action:

What is the craziest thing you've seen your loved one do?
Draw a picture or write a description.

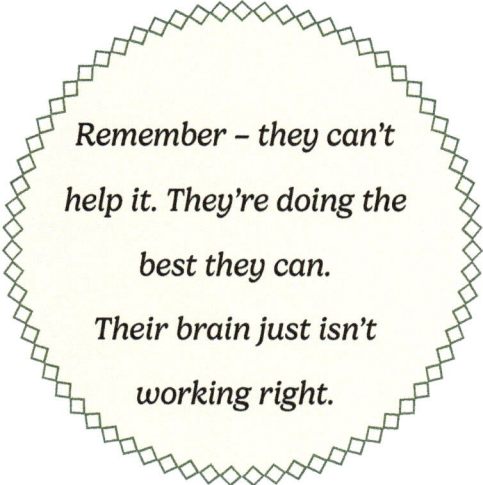

Remember – they can't help it. They're doing the best they can. Their brain just isn't working right.

Now I'm annoyed.
Why do I have to deal with this?

It's ok to be mad, or sad, or any other emotion you're feeling. I remember feeling all of those things many times. I felt sorry for myself too. I wanted to have fun being a kid, and not have my free time cut in half watching my dad.

My mom had to get a job to help pay bills and I think for other insurance and financial reasons too. (There is a lot of research and administrative work adults have to do to figure out how to manage with one less income.) Anyway, with mom working, it meant I had to be home more often to watch dad. It wasn't safe to let him stay home alone. It was stressful being 'in charge'. It was also boring. I was resentful that I couldn't go with my friends when they were out shopping or going to the movies, or to a football game. Sometimes I would get so mad, or sad, I would just cry. At least I didn't have to worry about

explaining it to my dad if he saw me. By this time, he didn't recognize that crying was unusual and he wasn't able to communicate, or speak in clear sentences. It's so mind-boggling to watch a person decline in this way, especially a parent.

Action: When you're feeling emotional or angry about the whole situation, take some time to write in a journal. Get all your feelings out. Say whatever you want because you never have to share it with anyone unless you want to. You'll be surprised how much it helps.

Journaling can be a great habit

to continue throughout your life.

Think of it as an easy form of therapy you can

do all on your own.

This is embarrassing.
What am I supposed to say?

I don't know about you, but I remember having friends over and my dad doing embarrassing things. Specifically, I remember being picked up by a guy in high school taking me out on a date. When he got to my house, he came in to get me and my dad was still up wandering around the house. (He was always wandering.) Anyway, Matt, the guy who I was going out with, came in and stayed for a while to be polite.

I remember we were playing a game at the kitchen table – I think Connect Four. My dad kept pacing around and around the house. He kept looking at Matt with a confused look in his eyes. I think maybe he had some idea what was going on . . . but not really. I imagine he didn't know what to do, but he kept staring. Matt was uncomfortable. I was uncomfortable. I couldn't wait to leave. Eventually he got aggressive and tried to accost Matt at the table. I was mortified. Thankfully, at that point, my mom became uncomfortable too and we quickly agreed it was time for us to go.

Action: Have you had an embarrassing moment like this? What happened? Did anyone else in your family see it? More importantly, did you talk about it later? If not, you should.

Tell me about it here . . .

Remember –
this is your book. Write
whatever you want and
only share it if you're
comfortable.

I feel guilty.
Why do we have to send him away?

We kept my dad at home as long as we could. Before he got Alzheimer's, he worked night shift a lot. I remember as a little kid he would often be sleeping in the day because he worked at night. My brother and I had to be quiet so we didn't wake him up. Now, he was home all the time and my mom had to work. She used to stay at home and take care of us. Now when she was at work, we took care of ourselves – and our dad. I tried to do my part, but it was becoming too much for me or my brother to manage - an adult who didn't understand what was appropriate and what wasn't, or what was safe and what wasn't. You know the story of cooking on the stove from before, he also didn't seem to like to wear clothes. Sometimes he would take them off and wander around the house in just his boxers. I didn't know what to think about that . . . or what to do. I wanted to hide. I wanted to pretend like it wasn't

happening. At least when my mom was there she would try to keep him dressed or keep me away. When it was just us, I didn't know what to do. I cried.

Sometimes he left the house. That was dangerous. Sometimes he wanted to drive. That was even more dangerous. In the end, there came a time when we couldn't manage it any more. We had people come to the house and help for a while, but soon even they couldn't manage the situation. My mom had to make the decision to put him in a care facility. It was hard for all of us. I felt so guilty that I couldn't do more. I know my mom must have felt that 100 times more.

Action: Write down the feelings you have if you're going through this, or write a letter to your family member. What would you want to say to them if you could have one more conversation?

_____

_____

_____

_____

_____

_____

_____

_____

_____

_____

_____

REMINDER: *it's ok to cry. Alzheimer's is super hard on everyone but remember, everyone is trying to do their best just like you are. Try to understand other perspectives and work together to support each other. Sometimes grown-ups need extra help and encouragement too.*

Sometimes I don't want to go visit . . I actually dread it.

I hate to say it, but it's been so much less stressful since my dad went away. I feel like a huge weight has been taken off my shoulders. I can breathe again. I can be a kid again. I can hang out with my friends again instead of staying home to watch dad. I feel terrible for thinking it, but it was such a burden and I didn't want to do it and I didn't want to miss out on my life to take care of his.

Now we go visit him at the care facility. It's not all the time, but it's every couple weeks (because he's out of town). I usually don't want to go. I feel SO guilty that I don't want to go, but it's true. I know he doesn't recognize me. I know it doesn't make a difference to him if I'm there or not. I don't like to see him like he is now. He doesn't know me and can't walk or talk or eat by himself. He's usually confined to the bed, or a chair for his safety. My mom tries to do the right thing. She wants to take us for his benefit even though she knows it doesn't matter. I think she still imagines he can see how we're growing, but in reality she knows he can't. We all go through the motions. I think it makes her feel better.

Action: If you're in a similar situation, please tell your parent, or another trusted family member, how you feel. You may still end up going because it's the 'right thing to do', but if you talk about it and share your feelings, maybe it will be a little bit easier.

REMINDER – Alzheimer's disease is cruel. It's hard. It's terrible. The only thing you have is the shared love for that person. Talk to those closest to you that are going through the same thing. They may be trying to be strong, but commiserating together is likely the best thing for everyone involved. Sometimes adults need help too. They try to shield you from hurt and don't realize that they're actually alienating you. You might have to be the one to make the first move.

The Alzheimer's Association is a fantastic organization to turn to for help. They have many resources for people of all ages. Check it out at alz.org

Why can't I just have a happy family like my friends?

I must have had this thought a thousand times. It's all I wished for. It seemed so unfair . . . and it is unfair. But unfortunately, life is often unfair. It may seem like your friends have an easier life or happier family – and maybe they do – but remember that looks can sometimes be deceiving. Pretty much every family has some sort of issue they're dealing with. It may not be as apparent, but I've never come across any family that didn't struggle with something. Try not to compare. I know it's hard, but there's little you can do to change the prognosis, so try to accept your situation and focus on the positives in your life.

Action: Make a list of all the positive things you have in your life. What are you thankful for? Thinking of the positives can help put you in a better mood and avoid a cycle of complaining or feeling sorry for yourself.

Studies show that thinking of things you're grateful for on a daily basis helps improve your mood and your mental health.

Why is this dragging on so long?

13 years. That's how long my dad lived with Alzheimer's disease. It's different for everyone, but in my case this lasted from the time I was 12 until I was 25, throughout all of my teenage years, college, marriage, and motherhood. Most of my memories of my dad are when he had Alzheimer's and not many are of him beforehand, but I have a few. I often wonder what it would have been like to know him as an adult, or how my life might have been different if he were actively involved as a father. I'll never know, but I'd like to think he would be proud of me now. He was never able to see his kids grow up, or enjoy retirement with my mom. I try to remember this isn't just something that happened to me. It happened to my whole family and it changed the course of all of our lives. While I have often blamed my dad's disease for negatively affecting me, the truth is that he was the victim. He was robbed of so much of his life.

Action: Spend as much time as you can thinking about happy memories you've had with your family member who has Alzheimer's. Relive them, feel the happy emotions. Share them with others. Burn them into your memory so you'll have them for the rest of your life. Write them down so you can read them back later and share them with your kids one day. Maybe even create a scrapbook.

Alzheimer's patients progress at different rates, have varying symptoms, and respond to treatments in many different ways. 13 years is on the very long side of the spectrum, so please don't assume your case will last as long.

I can't believe it's over

It's a funny thing. My family seems almost happy today. We're at lunch after the funeral and the conversation is pretty upbeat. Happy is the wrong word, it's more like relieved. I understand it. My dad has been in a nursing home for nearly a decade and most of that time he was unable to perform the most basic tasks of self-care. He didn't recognize any of his family, couldn't speak, and had no idea what was happening to him, or around him. For the rest of us, it was emotionally exhausting. Of course, we would all do anything to cure him, but knowing that was not an option, it always felt wrong to make him suffer in this way for so long.

Action: How do you feel about the passing of your loved one? Whether it has already happened or is yet to come, spend some time honestly thinking about your feelings around this topic. Think about it from your loved one's perspective as well. What would they think? I suggest talking this one through with someone you trust. There can be a lot of guilt around your feelings here, and it's best to talk it out if possible.

There's no right or wrong way to think or feel about this. The important part is coming to terms with your feelings. Talking with a therapist is a very healthy option if you're open to it.

What does this mean for me?

This is a tough one because the answer is: We don't know. My biggest fear is that I'll suffer the same fate as my dad. I've spent a lot of time thinking about it, reading about it, researching, etc. I try to follow the suggested lifestyle to lower my risk. But in the end, we don't know. I remind myself that nobody knows their fate or how their health will fare as they age. I think the best we can do is enjoy the life we have today. It's a blessing to have a healthy mind and body and we should take full advantage of that as long as we're able.

GIVE MEDITATION A TRY!

It's not for everybody, but you may find that it helps soothe your soul. If not meditation, try breathing exercises, or simply sitting quietly with your eyes closed. Giving yourself time and space to relax and calm yourself, thinking through your beliefs, setting goals or making plans for the future can all go a long way in relieving tension and anxiety.

More Journal Pages
To Write and Draw

Check out the
Alzheimer's Association.
It is a fantastic organization to
turn to for help. They have many
resources for people of all ages.

www.alz.org

www.ingramcontent.com/pod-product-compliance
Lightning Source LLC
Chambersburg PA
CBHW051649120626
46551CB00015B/2283